Colin Swatridge

A No-Nonsense Guide to Academic Writing

T0019574

Colin Swatridge

A NO-NONSENSE GUIDE TO ACADEMIC WRITING

Bibliographic information published by the Deutsche Nationalbibliothek

Die Deutsche Nationalbibliothek lists this publication in the Deutsche Nationalbibliografie; detailed bibliographic data are available in the Internet at http://dnb.d-nb.de.

Bibliografische Information der Deutschen Nationalbibliothek

Die Deutsche Nationalbibliothek verzeichnet diese Publikation in der Deutschen Nationalbibliografie; detaillierte bibliografische Daten sind im Internet über http://dnb.d-nb.de abrufbar.

Cover photo: ID 100744388 © Krittiraj Adchasai | Dreamstime.com

ISBN-13: 978-3-8382-1839-7

© *ibidem*-Verlag, Hannover • Stuttgart 2024

All rights reserved.

No part of this publication may be reproduced, stored in or introduced into a retrieval system, or transmitted, in any form, or by any means (electronic, mechanical, photocopying, recording or otherwise) without the prior written permission of the publisher. Any person who commits any unauthorized act in relation to this publication may be liable to criminal prosecution and civil claims for damages.

Alle Rechte vorbehalten. Das Werk einschließlich aller seiner Teile ist urheberrechtlich geschützt. Jede Verwertung außerhalb der engen Grenzen des Urheberrechtsgesetzes ist ohne Zustimmung des Verlages unzulässig und strafbar. Dies gilt insbesondere für Vervielfältigungen, Übersetzungen, Mikroverfilmungen und elektronische Speicherformen sowie die Einspeicherung und Verarbeitung in elektronischen Systemen.

Printed in the United States of America

A No-Nonsense Guide to Academic Writing

Contents

6

First Words

This guide is for students of social science and humanities subjects who are required to write long, or long-ish, essays. Students of the sciences will need to look elsewhere for guidance.

I have in mind, particularly, students at the undergraduate and master's levels who have received little guidance in the past; who may be studying in unfamiliar surroundings at home or abroad, where expectations may not be made clear – or clear enough; and mature students who may be returning to study after a break.

Why do I call this short book a 'no-nonsense' guide? Students don't have time, or inclination, to read any more than they need to, so I wanted to keep the text to the minimum. There are no test-yourself exercises of the sort that clutter many 'How to Write Essays' books. In spite of the fact that 'academic writing' is in the title, I take the view that writing at the college and university level need be no different from 'good', clear writing in other domains.

You really only need to read to the end of page 40. There are eleven line-drawings to break up the text somewhat; and even the examples that I give don't all have to be read. Of course, I hope you will read them; none of them is very long, and they're all by distinguished writers.

The second part of the book (page 41 onwards) consists of notes related to the language (but not only the language) you might be expected to use – or avoid using. These notes are sign-posted at relevant points in the main text. If you're confident about your English, you can probably read them selectively or not at all.

The essay/dissertation/thesis

You've a long essay, dissertation, or thesis to write – anything between three and three hundred pages of 'academic writing'. I shall use the word 'essay' throughout, because an essay is a dissertation or thesis on a smaller scale. In all of them, one argues a case.

I'm guessing that you've either not had to do this before, or you've not had to write so many words, or so many pages, as you're having to write now. You're expected to write in a formal, academic style – the very words 'thesis', and 'dissertation', suggest formality – and this may be off-putting.

What's so special about *academic* writing? Some would say it should be 'difficult'; it should use long words, in long sentences **[Note 1]**, like this:

> One critic has observed in Sibiescu's work the existence of a convergence correlation between the traditional and the modern: his expressionist poetics are said to be a generous synthesis of modernist avant-gardist art in respect of its form – setting it apart from tradition where its text rhetoric is concerned – but traditional in respect of its content, this being located, supposedly, in the ancestral foundations of our spirituality. The village, for Sibiescu, represents, as it were, a matrix space, where humanity reaches a plenitude, an ontological harmony, that surmounts the impasses and gnoseological aporias that make for alienation and a distancing from the 'mystery horizon'. Sibiescu's poetic universe converts the ontological status of the given real into the images of the paradisiacal or apollonian, evoking not merely the aesthetic, but also the existential sensibility.

Understood? Probably not, I scarcely understood it myself, at least on first reading. If the meaning of a text is unclear, if the language is almost wilfully unfamiliar, can we say it's well-written? Surely not.

Is this better?

> One critic notes the interplay of the traditional and the modern in Sibiescu's poetry. Where its form is concerned, Sibiescu's poetic style is both pioneering – parting company with an old-fashioned vocabulary and word-order – and traditional in respect of its

content. The poems, that is, are said to evoke the deep religious feelings of our ancestors. For Sibiescu, the village is the context in which we humans are most fulfilled, and we are most at ease. It is in the village, where difficulties are overcome, and we are most 'at home'. The world of Sibiescu's poems is one where nature is ordered, even heavenly; where there is both beauty and a real feeling of *being* to the full.

If I haven't entirely captured the meaning of the original, it just goes to show how teasing the worst kind of 'academic' writing can be. (I didn't know what to make of the 'mystery horizon'). Academics, especially, for whom English is the second language tend to write like this. You needn't, and shouldn't.

Still, there are some conventions you should bear in mind. You won't shorten 'will not' to 'won't, (as I'm doing in this guide); there won't be too much '*I* this', and '*I* that' **[Note 2]**; you'll use the same sort of language that you'll have come across in books and papers on your reading lists. It has a certain formality, an appropriate structure, and clear referencing – but that's about all there is to academic writing. **The important thing is to be clear.**

> Use technical terms where necessary, but avoid *jargon*. 'Academic writing' should be accessible to the intelligent general reader.

*

Another reason why writing a long essay may be off-putting is the length, and the time the job will take: the reading, the taking notes, the talking to people (including your supervisor), the management of your material. It may all look like a rather indigestible cake.

Cut the cake into slices – several slices – and chew your way through each without thinking about all those to come. The first slice will undoubtedly be the reading of books, journals, and websites that have something to say about the topic you've chosen to write about. This reading may well cause you to alter the focus of your topic.

The next will be to draft a review of what you've read – the parts of what you've read, that is – most relevant to your title. It may take a while to pin down that title. This isn't time wasted; but the sooner you have your title, the clearer it will be to you how much of what you read is relevant and how much isn't.

*

If you're an undergraduate student you might have been assigned to write this essay. Were you given a choice of titles, at least? If you weren't, can you modify the title you've been given? You may well think of a given title as an instruction to reproduce what's been written by all your student predecessors. If you were given a title like:

The causes of the American Revolution

You might well think that all you need to do is to read the standard histories and list the causes, one by one, more or less quoting or paraphrasing what you read. It's all been done before; that you should have to do it, too, is a nuisance, a hurdle, or series of hurdles, to jump over. That's probably what it feels like.

If you're a student at the master's level, you'll have a supervisor with whom you'll negotiate a topic and title. In some traditions, a **dissertation** is generally the end point of a taught course; and a **thesis** is a more or less book-length essay, the product of quite intensive research. In others, it's the other way round. An 'essay' at any level should have something fresh to say; at the postgraduate level, it should aim to break new ground.

You'll need to be really quite interested in the subject you've chosen. You may have to live with your choice of subject for quite a long time, so you must really want to find an answer to the question that's on your mind. If there's no such question you might as well play computer games.

I said that in an essay you argue a case. Let me argue this case:

> However short or long your essay, dissertation, or thesis needs to be, and whether or not you chose the title, it's yours – it's for you to shape it. There's no right shape, no pre-ordained shape. It's a cliché, but the more you put into it, the more you'll get out of it – and, more to the point, the better it'll be.
>
> Of course it's a chore if all you do is reproduce the thoughts of others; the point of writing an essay is to express thoughts of your own on the subject. It's your voice the reader wants to hear – or it should be. You're an adult: you've had thoughts and experiences to bring to the subject that others might not have had. Have the confidence to be a bit original.
>
> The word 'essay' comes from the French verb *essayer*, to try. An essay is a trial of ideas. You're presenting the thoughts of others, of course you are; but it's for you either to differ from them in some small way, or to add thoughts of your own – in short, to *interpret* what you've found. Do you agree in every respect with what others have said on the subject? It's unlikely. You won't push the boundaries of our knowledge and understanding very far; but in offering your own interpretation, writing the essay's less of a chore for you, and less of a chore for your reader.

What is an argument? It's a claim for which you make a case. The **main claim** in the above argument is the first sentence (in a short argument, it often is). That claim then needs to be supported by one or more further claims, or **reasons**. I reckon I've given five reasons for making it *your* essay.

*

(We hear a lot about 'large language models' [LLMs], or generative AI, and ChatGPT in particular. You might have been tempted to short-circuit the essay-writing process by having AI write it for you. AI can't make the sort of judgments that you will be called upon to make; and it certainly can't answer the questions that might be put to you, orally, by a human being, once you've submitted work that isn't yours).

*

Behind the older use of the word 'essay' is the notion of weighing, which we preserve in the word 'assay' – we speak of assaying precious metals (is this really gold? how many carats?). To write an essay is to weigh ideas in the balance so as to determine which is the weightier – which has the more support.

An 'academic' essay is a **debate**, not a manifesto **[Note 3]**. Your thoughts are the more telling when they counter-balance a position with which you disagree.

The reasons you give will need to be supported by **evidence** of some sort. I didn't give evidence for claims I made in the argument above; but (in a rather longer and perhaps more tedious argument) I might have drawn on personal experience **[Note 2]**: I've set essays, and examined them, at secondary, bachelor's, and postgraduate levels. I've read an awful lot of essays (some awful, most of them not).

The claims having been weighed, you come to a **conclusion**. My conclusion is in the final sentence ('offer your own interpretation') – again, it often is. I didn't prove or disprove anything, and nor will you. The most that can be hoped for is that your reader trusts you, and your handling of the evidence.

What follows is not prescriptive; it is suggestive. It is not *the* model of how to write a long essay; I hope, simply, to provide a route-map that you may find useful at the planning stage – a stage that may last quite a while and that, anyway, shouldn't be rushed.

> You shouldn't be writing this essay on your own, especially not if you're a postgraduate student: you have a supervisor to call on for help, and you've a right to expect that help. Your supervisor, though, has an equal right to expect you to be in the driving-seat.

The Title

Research – indeed, all knowledge – begins with a question: if there's no question, there's no answer, and no essay, no testing of ideas. Why might it be useful to frame the title as a question? I shan't argue for doing this – I'll simply give my reasons:

1. If you were presented with a title like 'The Idea of National Sovereignty', it would be difficult to judge where to begin and where to end.
2. A question ('What do we mean by sovereignty?') will help to determine what material is relevant – what goes some way to answering the question; and what isn't – what doesn't.
3. If it's your question you're answering ('Is sovereignty just another word for nationalism?'), the essay will be your answer, and not a mere re-presenting of others' answers.

The title of your essay need not be in the form of a question, but it will at least imply a question. Consider this title:

The advantages and disadvantages of a bicameral parliament

(A bicameral parliament is one that has two chambers, or two 'houses'). If the title 'The Causes of the American Revolution' might suggest that your essay will be in the form of a simple list, the above title might suggest two lists. In both cases, the result would be less an essay than a catalogue.

The issue might have occurred to you first as a question, e.g.:

Why should a parliament have two chambers?

If you're British, you might have wondered why there's a House of Lords (in which there are quite a lot of Ladies) in the Westminster parliament. The other three nations of the United Kingdom seem to manage with just one chamber. America has its Senate; France has its *Sénat*; Germany its *Bundesrat*. Why? Sweden, Finland, and Hungary have unicameral parliaments. Why? You'd need to look for reasons.

*

Here's an argument from an essay by Hilaire Belloc, member of parliament, writer of essays for a number of reviews, verse for children, and much else. He was writing in the 1920s and '30s:

The Crooked Streets

Why do they pull down and do away with the crooked streets, I wonder, which are my delight, and hurt no one?

Every day the wealthier nations are pulling down one or another in their capitals, and their great towns; they do not know why they do it, and neither do I.

It ought to be enough, surely, to drive the great broad highways which commerce needs and which are the arteries of a modern city, without destroying all the history and all the humanity in between – the islands of the past. The crooked streets are packed with human experience and reflect in a lively manner people's chances and misfortunes and expectations and homeliness and wonderment. One street marks a boundary, another the channel of an ancient stream, a third the track some animal took to cross a field, hundreds upon hundreds of years ago; another shows where a rich man's garden stopped long before the first ancestor his family can trace was born – the garden is now all houses, and its owner who took delight in it is just a name.

Leave people alone in their cities; do not pester them with the futilities of big government, or the fads of powerful men, and they will build you crooked streets, just as moles throw up mounds, and bees construct their honeycombs. There is no ancient city that does not glory, and that has gloried, in a multitude of crooked streets. There is no city, however devastated by government, if left alone, will not breed crooked streets in less than a hundred years and keep them for a thousand more.

Belloc is talking about the back-streets of old towns and cities, the chance result of unplanned circumstance. We'd probably talk about 'winding' streets now, rather than 'crooked' streets.

His title is a noun-phrase, but his first lines are a question. He's genuinely curious as to why characterful old streets should be bull-dozed by town-planners to create grids with ninety-degree intersections, as if all cities must be laid out like 'downtown' Manhattan. There's indignation in that question of his. It fires his essay.

*

There's another rather crucial point to be made about your title: **keep it tight**. Consider this one:

Britain and the slave trade

It's too big; too open-ended. Where would you start? Even if it was a question:

How big was Britain's involvement in the slave trade?

Or: How much of Britain's wealth was based on the slave trade?

it's still a big-book-length enterprise. The topic could be further refined by localizing it:

Is Bristol (or Liverpool, or Manchester) what it is now because of the slave trade?

Or by time-limiting it:

Was the end of the slave trade in 1807 the end of Britain's involvement in slavery?

The tighter your title, the more you set limits to the number of relevant sources you'll need to read, or otherwise take into account, and the more feasible your project will be. You'll be expected to have consulted a good spread of sources; still, the closer you stand up to a target the more likely it is you'll hit it.

> Don't give yourself too much to read; the careful analysis of well-chosen sources is more impressive than a pages-long bibliography of the barely relevant.

It's important that you ask a question that's researchable, given the resources (including the time) that's available; and that it's a question you really want an answer to. It might even be a question that hasn't been asked before in quite the way you ask it.

(Notes:

1. There's something to be said for not worrying too much about the precise words of your title until it's clear what shape the essay's going to take. You may want to change the title more than once so that it fits what you've actually written.
2. I use **sub-titles** in this text: in a long essay, you'll probably do the same, breaking your argument into 'chapters'. You might say what you intend to cover, at the beginning of each chapter, and what you hope to have shown, at the end.
3. Check what is expected in your institution concerning **format**: 12-point Times New Roman, 1.5 spacing, and justification at the right-hand margin are fairly standard settings.)

The Introduction

I was instructed at school to divide an essay into the Introduction, the Main Body, and the Conclusion. I never did find this a very useful break-down. It wasn't even obvious what the Introduction should include. But the 'main body' was the problem: this would account for at least 80 per cent of the whole thing (if we allow roughly – very roughly – 15 per cent to the Introduction, and 5 per cent to the Conclusion).

The introductory section might otherwise be called your **Statement of Intent**. It's where you say what you're going to do, how you're going to do it, and why.

The introduction, or statement, may take up just a single paragraph **[Note 4]** if you're writing an essay of a few pages; or several pages, if you're writing something longer. You might divide it into the following four parts (defining your terms; limiting your scope; stating your position; and describing your methodology).

Defining your terms

It may well be that your title – statement or question – contains a term that calls for some explanation. Indeed, sorting out what you mean by a word could affect whether your argument is persuasive or not. Consider this title:

Is assisted dying against nature?

Or, to put it another way:

Would it be an affront to nature to legalize assisted dying?

It might be necessary to point out at the start that 'assisted dying' is not 'mercy-killing' – indeed, that it's not *killing* at all. It's assisting the terminally ill (perhaps, for example, in the final stages of motor neurone disease) who wish to bring their dependent life to an end, but who can't do it for themselves. Strictly speaking, it is *doctor*-assisted dying that you'd be talking about.

Still more pivotal is how you'd define 'nature' – and this might depend upon whether you believe in 'supernature' – or God. If you do, your essay might be an attempt to show that assisted dying would be 'playing God': that it's not for us to determine our end when we have no choice at our beginning. If this is your line, you may have to accept that your argument will not persuade a non-believer.

It's best not to use a vague term like 'nature', at all. The title might be re-phrased thus:

Would doctor-assisted dying weaken our respect for human life?

You can't be too careful about your choice of terms, and how you'll define them for the purposes of your essay.

'Art', as in the following title, is another vague term that would need defining:

Is all art, like beauty, in the eye of the beholder?

Here are some attempts at defining it by painters and novelists:

Art has something to do with the achievement of stillness in the midst of chaos.
SAUL BELLOW

Art is a line around your thoughts.
GUSTAV KLIMT

Art is vice. You don't marry it legitimately, you rape it.
EDGAR DEGAS

Art always serves beauty, and beauty is the joy of possessing form, and form is the key to organic life since no living thing can exist without it.
BORIS PASTERNAK

Art is not truth. Art is a lie that that makes us realize truth.
PABLO PICASSO

Art does not reproduce the visible; rather, it makes visible. PAUL KLEE

Do not imagine that Art is something which is designed to give gentle uplift and self-confidence. Art is not a *brassière*. At least not in the English sense. But do not forget that *brassière* is the French for life-jacket.
JULIAN BARNES

Art is everything you can get away with.   ANDY WARHOL

The meaning of a word is in its use. Perhaps we've used the word 'art' **[Note 5]** to cover so many things we've emptied it of meaning.

Art? Craft? Design? An artless doodle?

Definition is hazardous. Dr Samuel Johnson in his pioneering *Dictionary* of 1755 had trouble with what might seem an easy word to define.

Thunder

> Thunder is a most bright flame rising on a sudden, moving with great violence, and with a very rapid velocity, through the air, according to any determination, upwards from the earth, horizontally, obliquely, downwards in a right line, or in several right lines, as it were in serpentine tracts, joined at various angles, and commonly ending with a loud noise or rattling.

Johnson was writing at a time when physics was still called Natural Philosophy – even so, you'd think Johnson would know the difference between thunder and lightning.

> If your essay title contains a term whose meaning is vague or contested, you'll need to be clear about how you'll use it.

Limiting your scope

Having refined your title and explained what you mean by it (if necessary), you may still want to limit the scope of the essay – and to be explicit about it **[Note 6]**.

'Science' is another term, like 'Art', that needs unpacking. Alan Isaacs was writing a 238-page book, but he was bound to leave out as much as he included:

Introducing Science

The subject of science has been expanding in all directions at such a rate during the last fifty years that, in order to produce a reasonably slender volume (...) it has been necessary to state the present view of the facts, with only a minimal reference to the historical sequence of their discovery or discoverers.

In a later book he confessed his own limitations:

The Survival of God in the Scientific Age

I have attempted to bring together some of the most interesting ideas from a variety of disciplines – physics, biology, psychology, philosophy, and theology (...). I have necessarily had to avoid trying to be exhaustive, so while I have certainly not told the whole truth, I hope that what I have said is nothing but the truth. Even in this respect, though, I am doubtful – as I was trained in only one of these disciplines, there will surely be lapses in the others.

There is a lot of 'I' in there; and perhaps Isaacs overdoes the self-effacement – but there will be limits to what you can cover in your essay, and it's as well to acknowledge this.

Sigmund Freud's *The Interpretation of Dreams*, published in 1900, has been called 'one of the most important books of the 20th Century'. Many writers before him had tried to solve the 'problem' of what our dreams might mean; but none could be said to have succeeded:

The Interpretation of Dreams

To write a worthwhile history of what we know and understand about our dreams is difficult, because no real progress has been made. No solid foundation of scientifically respectable results has been laid down, on which further investigation might build.

Every new author approaches the same problems afresh, and from the very beginning. If I were to enumerate such authors in chronological order, giving a survey of the opinions held by each of them, I should be quite unable to draw a clear and complete picture of the present state of our knowledge on the subject. I have therefore preferred to base my account on themes rather than authors.

I have not read the whole of this literature, since it is widely dispersed and contained in the literature on other subjects. Though I hope not to have overlooked any fundamental fact or important point of view therefore, the following survey cannot pretend to be exhaustive.

You won't be starting from scratch as Freud claimed to be doing; your chosen subject will likely rest on a pretty solid foundation of knowledge. This is all the more reason for limiting the scope of your enquiry as Freud did ('themes rather than authors').

You, too, may face the problem of a widely dispersed literature; so you, too, will have to be selective – and equally honest.

If you're writing to this title, for example:

The welfare state: has it been a success story?

You'll need to be clear about *where* it is you're writing about: England? The United Kingdom? The 'West'? You'll need to say *when* you'll take as a starting point: if you're focusing on the UK, will you begin with the 1908 Old Age Pension Act? Or with the Beveridge Report of 1942? How much time do you have? How long does your essay have to be? Wherever you start, your review will have to take in the present if you're to answer the question.

Or, perhaps, you'll write only about the welfare state as it concerns the elderly; or the unemployed; or people with disabilities. That's perfectly fine – as long as you make it clear that this is what you're going to do. Your reader knows you're not writing an exhaustive and definitive tome.

Stating your own position

In choosing your subject you'll already have an opinion about it. Some first-hand or second-hand experience of the welfare state might have nudged you one way or the other (success/failure). You'll have read some of the key documents on the subject – and they might have modified your opinion.

This is where you lay out your **main idea**, the case you want to argue. Let's imagine that you've been assigned **[Note 7]** this title:

Women and fiction

It's an unlikely title, but it's the title that Virginia Woolf was asked to speak about at two women's colleges at Cambridge, in 1928. How was she to interpret it? After much thought, she chose an alternative title:

A Room of One's Own

> But, you may say, we asked you to speak about women and fiction – what has that got to do with a room of one's own? (...) The title women and fiction might mean, and you may have meant it to mean, women and what they are like; or it might mean women and the fiction that they write; or it might mean women and the fiction that is written about them; or it might mean that somehow all three are inextricably mixed together and you want me to consider them in that light. But when I began to consider the subject in this last way, which seemed the most interesting, I soon saw that it had one fatal drawback. I should never be able to come to a conclusion. (...) All I could do was to offer you an opinion upon one minor point – a woman must have money and a room of her own if she is to write fiction. (...) If I lay bare the ideas, the prejudices, that lie behind this statement you will find that they have some bearing upon women and some upon fiction.

Woolf wrestled with what the scope of her lecture would be; but, having done so, she stated her position in simple terms: to write fiction in the 1920s, a woman must have money and privacy. It was a position based on her own experience as a writer, and, of course, she didn't regard it as a 'minor point' at all. Her audience might have expected her to talk about Jane Austen, George Eliot, or Louisa M. Alcott – this would have been, as it were, the **received opinion** (see below). Virginia Woolf had other ideas.

Suppose you ask yourself this question:

Should the role of the modern university be to prepare students for a career?

you probably find yourself thinking, intuitively, 'Yes, of course, why else would one go to university?', or 'No, a university is about much more than a job'. The position you take is your **hypothesis**. The point of the essay is to test it.

If your position is: 'Yes, that's what a university is for', I suggest you consider the opposite position ('No, it's to prepare one for *life*') before you justify your own.

Describing your methodology

Here, I shall be brief, since how you proceed will depend on your research question – and there is plenty of online guidance available[1]. Essentially, you'll need to explain:

- how you decided what information/data to collect
- where, and/or from whom, you collected it
- what use you made of it – how you analysed it.

Note the use of the past tense: by the time you've reached the final draft of your essay/dissertation/thesis you'll have done the above – for example, you might have explained that 'a random sample of 25 students was asked **[Note 7]** to agree or disagree (on a 5-point scale) with 25 statements quoted from relevant literature'.

You may, if you administer a questionnaire, or conduct interviews, collect **qualitative** (i.e. non-numerical) data. If so, you'll need to give an account, for example, of the questions you asked, how you selected those you questioned, and in what circumstances you questioned them

---

[1] https://gradcoach.co./what-is-research-methodology/; https://researchprospect.com/research-methodology/ are just two of the many relevant websites.

(face-to-face? online? over a period of weeks?). It may be that you will find yourself handling **quantitative** (statistical[2]) data.

> You may require a basic acquaintance with statistics – concepts and tests of correlation, significance, reliability, and so on – particularly if you are writing on a social science subject. Your supervisor is your first port of call for advice as to whether you need to manipulate numerical data.

You may decide to gather data by **observation** of people's behaviour (unobtrusively?), for example, as they drive, as they pass a homeless person, as they shop; or you may present one or more representative (anonymised?) **case-studies**; or draw on your own experience where this illustrates a point.

You'll almost certainly **consult documents**, printed or online – how many you consult, and quote, will depend on how tightly you've worded your question. Which ones you consult will depend on how *authoritative* you and others judge them to be (see **Sources**, below).

In short, in this methodology section, you should justify:

- what choices you made, and
- why.

---

[2] A useful basic guide to statistics is: www.thoughtco.com/what-is-statistics-3126367. Another is: tutorials.istudy.psu.edu/basicstatistics.

The Received Opinion

If you're writing a dissertation, or thesis, you'll be expected to review the literature on your topic. How much you have to read will depend, again, on how tightly you've worded your question; but you should aim to be familiar with the leading contributions to the field. These may or may not amount to one 'received opinion' – there may be a diversity of opinions on the issue. You'll likely side with one of these opinions against the others, for reasons of your own; or you'll add your own evidence to one or more of them.

You may, of course, find yourself disagreeing with all of them.

> Be sure to make a note, or write out a relevant quotation in full, when you come across something that relates to your title question – and record the details of the title of the source, its author, publisher, and the page numbers as you do so. You may not easily find them again. See below: **Note-making**.

Don't be afraid to disagree if you've good grounds for doing so. There's really no point in writing the essay at all if you're simply going to agree with what's been said or written before. (If you're writing at the undergraduate level, it might be enough to lay out the 'received opinion' in a systematic way, adding your own judgment by way of conclusion. Your supervisor should be able to advise whether, at the Master's level, this is enough).

*

Imagine you're given, or you choose, a title such as:

Is the rewilding of the countryside more than simple nostalgia?

You might be tempted to respond, straight away: 'Yes of course it is! We need to restore as much as possible of the biodiversity we've lost'. Before you do this, though, consider the case for *not* rewilding.

Let's imagine that you find four sources that argue *against* rewilding:

1. Rewilding the UK's beautiful moorland would be a mistake. Our moors are a unique habitat for many species of birds; and moorland peat absorbs more carbon dioxide than any number of trees.

2. Reintroducing wolves to the Welsh uplands would devastate sheep-farming: Welsh lamb is – or has been – a vital export commodity. The thin soils of upland Wales are good for little else than for sheep-grazing.

3. Wild boar and elk cannot be allowed to roam in a landscape that we humans have sanitized. We could not easily accommodate species like these on managed land; they would need to be fenced in if they weren't to be a danger to livestock.

4. There are many examples of the negative effects of introducing non-native species into an ecosystem. When Canadian beavers, for instance, were introduced to the southern tip of South America they chewed their way through virgin forest.

The order in which to place different items is often a puzzle. If you have dates for each case, it would make sense to adopt a **chronological order**. Another order might be **thematic**, where you give examples whose impact is *economic*; others where it's *environmental*, or *social*, and so on. Or you might present the examples in order of **significance**: the costs (financial; lost alternative opportunities) and benefits (financial, human, and ecological).

Having presented a range of negative views, it would be as well to summarize the case for *not* rewilding before presenting your counter-argument.

Why look at the opinion(s) with which you may disagree first? **[Note 3]**. In doing so you show that:

a) you know and understand what it is you're disagreeing with, or adding to;
b) you accept that there's more than one reasonable point of view;
c) you've found something in, or absent from, the received opinion(s) that your own argument will counter-balance, or your own evidence will modify, in some way.

*

Poet Edmund Blunden begins **[Note 8]** an essay on villages in England by considering cities:

English Villages

It is possible to fall in love with England's great cities: I have met people from across the Channel who even looked back to their time in the dingiest parts of London with enthusiasm and gratitude. There was certainly more than nostalgia for earlier years and scenes in their appreciation. These friends of London had discovered not only how many surprises there were in almost every part of it, but the extraordinary cheerfulness and frankness of the people in whatever circumstances. It is not for me to praise London or Londoners, or to discuss other of the larger cities in Great Britain, but it must be admitted that in spite of everything, our cities have a way of making friends.

However this may be, I am persuaded that whoever wishes to find the best in this country, should look in the English village. This is, of course, a generalization that covers an astonishing variety of scenes and qualities and experiences; but the visitor is rewarded mentally and emotionally by the treasures to be found. The sheer individuality of any one village gratifies the senses. The very names of so many English villages testify to a rich history of farming practices, of lords in their manors, and the centrality of the Church. A Japanese friend, as we were following a path across the hayfields and the old cricket ground, noticed a stately house encircled with a moat. He asked me what it was. "The vicarage – the parson's house", I said. He repeated my words with a smile of wonder. I think it was the first time he had really appreciated what a solid and dignified little world the English village is.

This is an edited version of what Blunden wrote back in 1942. What's interesting about it, for our purposes, is that he looks at cities, briefly, first, before praising the virtues of the English village.

Barbara Ward (in *The Home of Man*[3]) does something similar when she writes **[Note 8]** about high-rise apartment buildings:

The Search for Community

[Tower blocks] were the public authorities' first response to the destruction of war or the need to replace increasingly decrepit housing, or the combination of both. The aim, undoubtedly, was well-intentioned. Slum-dwellers would be rescued from overcrowding, bad air, bad light, dirt, noise, and the absence of domestic services by receiving modern apartments in fine new tower blocks, all air and light, with wide open spaces round them and a measure of insulation from the traffic, noise and disturbance of the streets.

But it is precisely this anonymity and insulation that feed the fears. Over those wide, windy spaces, into those entrances serving over a hundred families, up those deserted elevators and along the connecting corridors, anybody can roam and no one can be certain whether it is neighbour or enemy – particularly if vandals have removed the house lights and broken the elevator. All these reactions taken together – the sense of being dwarfed, helplessness, segregation, anonymity and fear – make one thing clear. From London to New York to St Louis to Holland's Bijlmermeer to *Grands Ensembles* in Paris, a massive commitment

---

[3] © International Institute for Environment and Development, 1976

to high-rise housing for poorer citizens is a failure, an expensive, corrosive, tragic failure.

Again, I have edited the original so as to bring out **[Note 9]** the contrast between the 'received opinion' and the writer's argued response to it.

A good essay opposes one position to another, as in a debate. Blunden contrasts the city with the village; and Ward pits the advantages of the high-rise apartment building against its manifest social drawbacks. The difference is that, in an essay, you are the spokesperson on both sides. The temptation might be to caricature the received opinion – to make a 'straw man' of it: an easy target. You would not strengthen your counter-argument if you did this; on the contrary, by making a 'steel man' of the position you're countering, you'll need to make sure **[Note 9]** your position is the more persuasive.

Sources

What sources you use – what sources are relevant – will, of course, be determined by the question you choose to address. You might decide to write a long essay to this title:

What lessons for the future did we learn from the COVID-19 pandemic?

I choose this topic merely to illustrate some of the hazards to be aware of when selecting your sources – that's all. I am not qualified to take a position on the science.

If numbers are what we're looking for, we'd be well advised to turn to the Office for National Statistics (ONS). It's independent of government, but is recognized to be the UK's most thorough population data-bank; so, when on its website[4] we read:

'Of the deaths involving COVID-19 that occurred in England and Wales in March to June 2020, there was at least one pre-existing condition in 91.1% of cases.'

We can be pretty sure that it's as accurate a figure as we're likely to get – once, that is, we have accepted the UK definition of a 'death' in this context as one that occurred within 28 days of a positive test result.

The British Medical Journal (BMJ) is a reliable source for the up-to-the-minute thinking of medical professionals. More than 50 million users from over 150 countries access its websites every year. So, when associate editor Peter Joshi wrote[5], (asking whether the influenza vaccine had taught us anything about the efficacy of a coronavirus vaccine):

'Sixty years after influenza vaccination became routinely recommended for people aged 65 or older in the US, we still don't know if vaccination lowers mortality. Randomized trials with this outcome have never been done.'

we knew we could take him seriously, because we knew his peers had done so.

The Danish mortality monitoring network, EuroMOMO, is supported by the European Centre for Disease Prevention and Control (ECDC), and by the World Health Organization (WHO). Like the ONS, it collects statistics – but from 27 European countries[6]. It could safely be regarded as an **authority**, alongside the ONS and BMJ.

We should be rather more careful when it comes to websites hosted by **individuals**. Dr Malcolm Kendrick, for instance, advertised himself on his blog[7] as a 'Scottish doctor, author, speaker, sceptic...living in

---

[4] www.ons.gov.uk/peoplepopulationandcommunity/healthandsocialcare/conditionsanddiseases

[5] www.bmj.com/content/371/bmj.m4058

[6] www.euromomo.eu

[7] www.drmalcolmkendrick.org

Macclesfield.' This might not have given immediate assurance; but he did, at least, admit to consulting EuroMOMO.

We may wonder what authority Toby Young could claim, as a journalist and occasional playwright, who was sacked by *Vanity Fair*, and wrote a restaurant column for the *Evening Standard*. His website, *lockdownsceptics.org*, states his position straight away; but he claimed to be unfriendly towards conspiracy theories. He might have been thinking of those of Dr Vernon Coleman, who on one[8] of his many websites, noted that, thanks to COVID-19:

'The EU's long-term plan to get rid of small businesses will be successful at last.'

This is a man with fixed, ill-informed opinions.

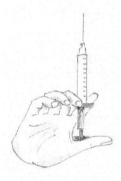

Though the 'World Doctors Alliance' (WDA) looks as though it would be a global organization, it was founded only in September 2020, by Dr Mohammad Adil, a consultant general surgeon. (Among the eight members listed on its website[9] is a dentist, a psychiatrist, and Dr Vernon Coleman). The claim was made in Dr Adil's 'open letter' to the world that:

'Had hydroxychloroquine (HCQ) been available there would not have been a pandemic.'

---

[8] www.vernoncoleman.com/coronavirusscare.htm
[9] www.worlddoctorsalliance.com/

Another indication of whether a document can be relied on or not is its **date of publication**. The above claim, for example, concerning the efficacy of hydroxychloroquine, was made before the founding of the WDA, in January 2020. This notice was published on a UK government website[10], six months later, in June 2020:

'*The Medicines and Healthcare Products Regulatory Agency (MHRA) took into consideration the results released from the RECOVERY trial showing no beneficial effect of HCQ in patients hospitalized with COVID-19.*'

(Note: HCQ has proved to be effective against malaria, rheumatoid arthritis and certain other conditions – but not COVID-19).

The claim that: 'The evidence (...) indicates that there should be no expectation of a large second wave', on the *lockdownsceptics.org* website, was dated 8 September 2020. Just ten days later, the BBC[11] carried this message:

'*The UK is "now seeing a second wave" of COVID–19 Prime Minister Boris Johnson has said, adding "it's been inevitable we'd see it in this country".*'

Inevitable or not, it happened; so, when Mike Yeadon, writing on the same website on 21 October 2020 wrote: 'the pandemic is effectively over and can easily be handled by a properly functioning NHS', it was not long before Professor Stephen Powis at a Downing Street briefing on 18 January 2021[12], said:

'*We are seeing extreme pressure [on the NHS], more than we've ever seen before, more than the first peak.*'

So, the **later** your information is, as well as the more reliable, the better.

Still, articles written by even only one named author are **[Note 10]** preferable to one that's **anonymous**. It may be honest, but it doesn't encourage trust, when an author states at the outset on his website[13]:

---

[10] www.gov.uk/government/news/mhra-suspends-recruitment-to-
covid...
[11] www.bbc.co.uk/news/uk-54212654
[12] www.bbc.co.uk/news/av/uk-55705495
[13] www.inproportion2.talkigy.com/pages/about.html

'I am a concerned citizen from the UK who has had a varied career in a number of occupations (...) I am neither a scientist nor medic.'

Whoever he is he does have the goodness to warn his readers to be sceptical and to think for themselves. This is more than can be said for a 'small group of people in the UK with families and careers across sectors including technology and engineering, retail, fitness, and the service industries', who professed to be 'ordinary British people who were concerned about the direction the UK was heading in response to COVID-19'. They didn't identify themselves, except under the title: *Evidence Not Fear*[14].

> It's the anonymity of *Wikipedia,* incidentally, that rules it out as a dependable source. Turn to it for information of an uncontroversial kind – dates, names, basic biographical details; but don't quote from it, or cite it as a source.

Finally, you should treat with special caution a source that makes wild claims and uses **language** in extravagant ways. Vernon Coleman, (who besides denying the reality of AIDS, and of global warming), referred to COVID-19 as:

'The Greatest Hoax in History. The startling truth behind the planned world takeover.'

And Malcolm Kendrick, gave it as his opinion that 'the world has simply gone bonkers'. He questioned the way in which several countries (including the UK) defined deaths from COVID as those that occurred within 28 days of a positive test result. 'I don't know much for sure about COVID-19', he writes, 'but I do know that is just complete nonsense'. He accused all governments of 'floundering about' and ignoring evidence. 'In truth,' he said, 'they have achieved nothing.'

Downright judgements of this sort belong in popular newspapers and blogs, not in essays long or short.

---

[14] https://evidencenotfear.com/

In conclusion, when an issue is as current, and as fast-developing as COVID-19 was, it's vital that you have access to the most recent information, coming from a well-established institution (a university, a democratic government, a respected thinktank), or a trustworthy, named, individual who uses language **[Note 10]** with care.

Note-making

You'll be reading always with your question in mind. If it's a book, the contents page, and index, will take you to what's relevant; it isn't always necessary to read the whole book. As you read, you will need to keep track of what you want to quote, paraphrase, or otherwise refer to. You're looking for connections among the sources: where they agree with each other (and with you), and where they disagree.

It might be as well to break your question into sub-topics. Let's suppose your question is:

There is a minimum wage; can a case be made for a maximum income?

The sub-topics might be as follows:

- the *welfare* basis for the minimum wage
- the *fairness* case for a maximum income
- the *mechanism* by which a maximum might be imposed
- the *reward*-for-enterprise argument
- the practical *obstacles* to regulation

These sub-topics might then be inserted, vertically, into a matrix such as the following, where documents are placed horizontally:

	Thomas (2016)	Swift (2019)	Berwald (2021)
welfare	p. 30: 'The Labour government of Tony Blair introduced the National	pp.49-51: There was a good deal of opposition to the new law on the part of employers, big	p. 121: Most European countries have introduced minimum-wage legislation on

	Minimum Wage in 1998 in the interest of social justice in the UK'	and small	welfare grounds
fairness	p. 32: There was a recognition that gross inequalities caused discontent among the 'left behind'	p. 52: 'A balance had to be struck between the supposed rights of employees, and the finances of small businesses'	p.123: 'By July 2021, 21 out of 27 EU countries had introduced a national minimum wage'
mechanism	p.39: 'In San Francisco, voters approved a plan to levy a 0.1% tax on companies whose CEO was awarded more than 100 times the company's median income'	p.54: Remuneration committees of big companies will always find ways of paying executives 'incentive' salaries, in a global market for top managers	pp.130-131: No way of limiting 'excessive' pay awards has yet been found – but salary levels in EU countries are not on the same scale as in the US
etc.	etc.	etc.	etc.

You'll be referring to many more than just three sources, so your matrix would extend horizontally. You might need to allocate a fresh page for each source. Some cells in any such matrix might, of course, be empty. Some sources will only give you useful evidence in respect of one or two sub-topics.

Your notes might not be in full sentences as above: the important thing is to **distinguish between what you're quoting, and what you're paraphrasing.** (Apologies in advance if I make this point again).

I make no claim to the originality of this matrix suggestion – and that's all it is: a suggestion. You may have your own way of managing your notes.

Quotation

You will want to quote the actual words used by writers of the sources you apply to, as I have done in the above section. In representing what I'm calling 'the received opinion' you'll want to quote some of the actual words used by those who have contributed 'answers' to your question – as you will when you come to write your counter-argument.

Why will you quote?

These are perhaps the most obvious reasons for making direct quotation:

1. The sentence, or the passage, that you quote is from a particularly authoritative source, and would be recognized as such by your reader;
2. It either expresses, in a nutshell, what you're arguing against, or it gives very strong support to your argument;
3. It makes its case well, and clearly, so that you may feel you couldn't improve on it.

The young Simone de Beauvoir wasn't writing a thesis, to be sure, when she quoted the French novelist and politician Maurice Barrès; but the words she quotes in this extract met all three of the above criteria, when, no longer a child, she quarrelled with her parents:

Memoirs of a Dutiful Daughter

The most innocent conversations concealed traps: my parents translated my comments into their own idiom, imputing ideas to me that were simply not mine. I was always being cornered by the meanings of words. In this situation I thought of what Barrès had written: 'Why these words, this brutal precision which over-simplifies our complexities?'. As soon as I opened my mouth I made a rod for my back, and was caged again in a cell that I had spent years trying to escape, where everything, without question, had its name, its place, and its function.

De Beauvoir has placed single inverted commas round the embedded *written* quotation, which is the usual practice. Double inverted commas are placed round words that have been *spoken* – where they're genuinely 'speech-marks' – as de Beauvoir does here:

He quoted to me the subject of a dissertation with which teacher-trainees teased themselves: "The difference between the notion of concept and the concept of notion". He had thought up similar titles, though, in fact, his association with the university was rather remote.

Double inverted commas are also used for a quotation within a quotation. But it may be policy where you are to use singles only, or doubles only.

*

How much quotation should there be? Again, your own university/faculty/department might have its own policy on this, among other matters (how quotations should be punctuated, how many and how long they should, or shouldn't be), so nothing that I say here – as elsewhere – should be taken to override such a policy.

> As a general rule: don't let the amount of quotation exceed the amount of your own discussion. **What is vital is that your reader can easily tell the difference between what is yours, and what isn't.**

The length of any one quotation will depend on which of the three reasons for quoting applies. If it's a fairly short, sentence-length, quotation it can be embedded in your text: thus, for example, I might claim the backing of Watson who wrote: 'To quote briefly an authority on the subject pays her a pretty compliment, but to overdo it is stealing' (Watson, 2019: p. 43).

If, however, it's a longer quotation, of, say, 30 words or more, it's advisable to separate it from your own words; to skip a line, and to indent it. Thus, Watson wrote a little more expansively:

> Perhaps to call over-quotation 'stealing' is an over-statement; but it is all too easy to fall into the way of quoting at unnecessary length, in order to add to the word-count, or to make up the required number of pages. Of course, this isn't plagiarism, where the student tries to pass off other people's writing as his own; but

it might amount to a rather aggressive borrowing (Watson, 2019: p. 44).

Inverted commas aren't needed at all around such a longer, indented quotation.

Your coverage of the 'received opinion' (as expressed, we'll assume, by multiple authors), or your 'review of the literature' bearing on your question, is where you're representing the views of others: so, you may well quote more here than you will when it comes to mounting your counter-argument.

References

I made reference only to websites in the section on Sources; it takes a while before **[Note 11]** authors and publishers issue books on matters that take time to research and make safe judgments about. So, if you're looking for the latest research articles, and criticism of them, you'll find them online.

Your institution may well have a subscription to relevant, online and paper copies of journals; but thousands of journals are to be found online that you can read free of charge[15].

When you quote any number of words from a source of any kind you need to make it clear where it comes from. The commonest referencing convention is the **Harvard** system; and this is the one I use, as below. Others are the Chicago system; the Modern Language Association (MLA), and the American Psychological Association (APA) conventions. Ask your supervisor which referencing convention you should use.

Where you paraphrase an author's words, and the author is named, it is enough to bracket the **date** of publication after the author's name:

> Did the Greeks call themselves philosophers? Sumner (2017), for one, doubts it: it seems that the label was pinned on Pythagoras much later, to mean that he was simply a 'seeker after wisdom'.

---

[15] Three such open sources are: Google Scholar (https://scholar.google.co.uk); Academia (https://academia-edu); and Research Gate (https://www.researchgate/net).

When you don't name the **author** in your text, the name goes in brackets before the date of publication:

> Did the Greeks call themselves philosophers? The label might have been given to them only later. There is no evidence, for example, that Socrates thought of himself as anything more than a teacher (Sumner, 2017).

When you include a brief, direct quotation in the text, the **page** number is added:

> It is a question whether the Greeks actually called themselves philosophers. Sumner doubts it: 'There is no evidence that Socrates, for example, called himself a philosopher, thinking of himself simply as a teacher' (Sumner, 2017: p. 43).

A reader will expect to find 'Sumner' in your **bibliography**, alphabetically ordered by author **[Note 12]**. Every reference in the text should find its counterpart there; and every document listed in the bibliography should have been signposted in the text.

> It isn't enough to list your sources in the bibliography: there needs to be a reference to the source of every quotation or paraphrase as it occurs.

The entry in your bibliography simply gives readers the information needed to find the document for themselves should they wish to do so: author, date, title, place of publication, publisher.

Sumner, Eric (2017) *The Beginnings of Philosophy*. London, UK: Routledge

If you're referring to an article in a journal, you'd give the author's name, as before, in the text, but you'd enter the item in the bibliography as follows:

Bradley, Stephen (2021) Atonal music: a wrong turning. In *The Musicologist*, Vol. 15, No. 3, pp. 46-56

If it's an essay in a collection of essays, it can be entered thus:

Bradley, Stephen (2021) Atonal music: a wrong turning. In: Ian Skelton (ed.) *Twentieth-Century Music Making*. Cambridge, MA: Harvard University Press

And if it's an article posted online, it might appear thus:

Bradley, Stephen (2012) Atonal music: A Wrong Turning. Available from: www.themusicologist.com/31/mar/2021/atonal-music-a-wrong-turning.htm [Accessed 18th July 2021][16]

It might be the convention to separate websites from printed documents, or to integrate them. Either way, the author's name is always the entry term. It might not be one author, of course; and it might not be a person, but an institution.

It little matters which convention you use where referencing is concerned (as long as it's approved by your supervisor), and that it's **clear** and **consistent**.

> It's important that **whatever you borrow is distinguishable from what is yours**. Your own voice is what your reader wants to hear – or it should be.

---

[16] A full explanation of the Harvard system is available from: www.imperial.ac.uk/admin-services/learning-support/reference-management/harvard-style/your-reference-li...

You might at this stage reach an intermediate conclusion,

- briefly acknowledging that the material you've reviewed has some merit,
- but pointing out weaknesses in it,
- and looking ahead to how you'll support the position you've taken in your introduction.

Your Counter-Argument

Now you're ready to lay out the case you outlined in your introduction. You've taken the 'received' case seriously; you've weighed it in the balance; now your own case needs to be heavier.

Bear in mind that you see any topic from a particular angle. Each of us has a certain upbringing, and a certain set of experiences. These combine to make a unique individual of you, and to lend you an either slight or pronounced **bias**. At the extreme, it amounts to a prejudice. Oliver Goldsmith, in 1760, found himself in male company in an unnamed pub or coffee-house:

On National Prejudices

Amongst a multiplicity of other topics, we took occasion to talk of the different characteristics of the several nations of Europe; when one of the gentlemen, cocking his hat, and assuming such an air of importance as if he had possessed all the merit of the English nation in his own person, declared that the Dutch were a parcel of avaricious wretches; the French a set of flattering sycophants; that the Germans were drunken sots, and beastly gluttons; and the Spaniards proud, haughty, and surly tyrants; but that in bravery, generosity, clemency, and in every other virtue, the English excelled all the world.

I told him that, for my part, I should not have ventured to talk in such a peremptory strain unless I had first made a tour of Europe, and examined the manners of these several nations with great care and accuracy.

Few of us are quite as opinionated as the English bulldog in Goldsmith's company, or as downright; but it's as well to be aware of what assumptions you might make – where your opinions come from, and where your own bias might lie. You mustn't be shy about voicing your own opinion: 'opinion' is really only another word for 'judgment' – and your judgment is certainly called for. Save it for the end, though.

Evidence

Goldsmith was reluctant to express his opinion, but when asked for it, he did – and it wasn't well received. But, of course, he was right to want evidence on which to base his opinion. The word *evidence* comes from the Latin 'to see': evidence is what we can see; it's out there, visible to all. Consider that earlier question:

Is the rewilding of the countryside more than simple nostalgia?

If you were to counter the arguments against re-wilding **[Note 13]**, you'd need better evidence of its success than its opponents managed to assemble of its failures. What might you find?

1. The Red Kite was an endangered species in the UK, until 13 young birds were introduced to the Chiltern Hills. Since then, numbers have surged. The Royal Society for the Protection of Birds has called it 'the biggest species success story in UK conservation history'.

2. Less fertile farmland in the Côa Valley, in Portugal has been abandoned. As the population has dropped, so wolves and Iberian lynx have been reintroduced, and now thrive there.

3. Beavers were hunted to extinction in the UK. In 2009, a family of beavers was released in Knapdale Forest, Argyll, Scotland, and there are now colonies in Devon, and in Wales, bringing biodiversity and enhanced water quality.

4. *Bilbies* are marsupials (mammals carried by the mother when young) like kangaroos and koalas. They had not been

seen in New South Wales national parks for a century, until 50 adults were released into a predator-free area in 2019 by the Australian Wildlife Conservancy.

Do these positive stories outweigh the negative stories in the 'received opinion'? They seem merely to counter-balance them. Something more is needed. There is the famous case of the reintroduction of wolves to the Yellowstone National Park, in 1995, and the positive effects this had on other species[17]. That was called by scientists 'one of the greatest rewilding stories the world has ever seen'. But perhaps an example of rewilding that benefited people as well as an ecosystem is a still greater success. It concerns the translocation of a herd of a species of Asian wild ass, the *kulan*, to a southern Ukraine steppe, 50km north-east of the Danube delta. Pernilla Hansson, in a blogpost, writes[18]:

> The kulan could form an additional prey species for predators such as wolves and golden jackals, and their grazing will keep grass length on the steppe short, which not only mitigates wildfire risk, but also benefits endangered steppe residents, such as the souslik [a European ground squirrel], dependent on open grasslands.

> The people living in the Danube Delta region are often socioeconomically vulnerable, and its rewilding provides new sources of income, not only through tourism, but also through sustainable harvesting of revitalized plant and animal populations.

It isn't a knock-out blow, exactly: but it adds a benefit to local people to the benefits to wildlife. It answers the question with a quite resounding: Yes, there is more to rewilding than simple nostalgia.

> It's easiest to place the entire 'received opinion' first, followed by the entire response to it. But you may prefer to interleave points (for and against) as in a formal debate. There's no one right structure.

---

[17] 'A Rewilding Triumph', by Cassidy Randall, in *The Guardian*, 25 January 2020.
[18] https://overpopulation-project.com/a-decreasing-population-furthers... 26/08/20

Examples

Any claim, any opinion, needs grounding in evidence; if that evidence is truly to be 'seen', it has to consist of examples. Well-chosen examples will persuade where assertion, by itself, will fall flat.

H. L. Mencken was an American essayist and humourist. He was not afraid of making some pretty bold claims. I have omitted some of the florid language used in this argument from 1918:

In Defense of Women

Men know how to sweat and endure. Men are amiable and fond. But insofar as they show the true fundamentals of intelligence, to that extent at least, they are feminine. Find me an obviously intelligent man, a man of the first class, and I'll show you a man with a wide streak of woman in him. Bonaparte had it; Goethe had it; Schopenhauer had it; Bismarck and Lincoln had it; Shakespeare had it. The essential traits and qualities of the male are, at the same time, the hallmarks of the Schalskopf. **[Note 14]**

It would be an easy matter, indeed, to demonstrate that superior talent in man is practically always accompanied by this feminine flavour – that complete masculinity and stupidity are often indistinguishable.

The truth is that neither sex, without some fertilization by the complementary character of the other, is capable of the highest reaches of human endeavour.

Mencken gives us six examples of men who had a 'wide streak' of the feminine in them – at least, this is what he tells us. Perhaps, to be persuaded by his argument, we'd need to be shown in what respects, for example, Shakespeare gave evidence of his feminine side.

Was it the fancy collar (or ruff), or the long hair spilling over it?

Mary Coleridge was writing in the late 1800s. Here, she writes about explorers in general; but she praises one in particular – a woman like herself – Isabella Lucy Bird, the first woman to join the Royal Geographical Society, in 1892: **[Note 15]**

Travellers' Tales

What fine fellows are the great explorers from Columbus to Greeley! With what magnificent chivalry do they go forth to fight the sun, the sea, the snow, that they may win new lands, new light for the world! To travel anywhere intelligently is to discover for yourself, if not for anyone else; and the undiscovered country lies not only in the heart of Africa, nor round the Poles. Who, for instance, discovered Yorkshire before Charlotte Brontë?

There are people who ought to be paid to travel, they do it so well. Miss Bird is one of these. She is such excellent company in Japan, that we could almost find it in our hearts, even at the end of her two fat volumes, to wish she had stayed there a month longer. Hers are no sentimental journeys; she does not burst into lyrics, and nobody ever tries to murder her; but she has good eyes, and she uses them. And then, Miss Bird is such a charming name for a traveller! Fate clearly had something to do with it. Heresy though it be to say so, her travels are much better reading than Goethe's.

Mencken used the word 'truth' in his conclusion. This is a word to be treated with caution. He claims that nobody really achieves at the highest level if they aren't a mixture of the masculine and the feminine. It's a generalization **[Note 16]**, and there may be some truth in it. His examples give support to his claim; but it's still a claim – it isn't 'the truth'.

Facts

It isn't a fact, either. A fact is either what is discovered to be the case, or it's the case by definition. That nuclear fusion has not provided us with a reliable source of electrical energy is a fact by discovery; that the first-born of the British monarch is heir to the throne is a fact by definition.

But facts may change: we may yet manage to build an efficient nuclear-fusion reactor; and it is a fact that before 2011 the first-born *son* of the monarch was heir to the throne. The law was changed to allow a daughter to be first in the line of succession. There are no facts in the Mencken argument; and there are few in Mary Coleridge's.

Mark Twain does give us some facts in the passage below. He was keen to show that America is older than we may think:

Life on the Mississippi

The world and the books are so accustomed to use, and over-use, the word 'new' in connection with our country that we get the impression that there is nothing old about it. De Soto, the first white man who ever saw the Mississippi River, saw it in 1542. The date 1542 standing by itself, means little or nothing to us, but when one groups a few neighbouring historical dates and facts around it, he realizes that this is one of the American dates which is quite respectable for age.

For instance, in 1542 Michelangelo's paint was not yet dry on the Last Judgment in the Sistine Chapel; Mary Queen of Scots was not yet born, but would be before the year closed; Catherine de Medici was a child; Elizabeth of England was not yet in her teens; Shakespeare was not yet born.

Unquestionably, the discovery of the Mississippi is a fact which considerably modifies the shiny newness of our country and gives her a most respectable antiquity.

We are given, perhaps, six indisputable facts in this short argument – one is pretty safe where dates are concerned. Mark Twain is careful to call De Soto the 'first *white* man' to see the river; he is less careful when he calls 'the discovery of the Mississippi' in 1542 a 'fact'. The fact is that there were several Native American tribes in the region, long before 1542, who'd seen the river and given it its name.

The evidence that you present to support your counter-argument will need a factual underpinning. Make sure, though, that they really *are* facts.

Conclusion

It would be as well to write a **short summary** of what you've done, before coming to a final judgment. Let's take the rewilding title again to provide an example of the sort of summary you might write:

> The issue is whether there is more to rewilding than simple nostalgia. I took the position that there is: that, where it is suitable, and it is carefully monitored, the benefits outweigh the risks.
>
> I considered the case for not rewilding and pointed out weaknesses in it. In particular, it was shown that failures were the result of having chosen an unsuitable ecosystem; or the introduction of an unsuitable species; and not having completed a thorough risk assessment, in order to avoid unintended consequences.
>
> In my counter-argument, I presented evidence of rewilding initiatives that had desirable outcomes precisely because objectives worked with the grain of nature; the ecosystem and species were well chosen; and local people shared the project's objectives, and benefited from the outcomes.
>
> I, therefore, conclude that...

You stated your position in your introduction. This was your 'answer' to the question in the title; your hypothesis, or – less grandly – your intuitive point of view. You might draw an intermediate conclusion here: having reflected on the evidence you've presented. Did it all point in one direction?

As you reviewed how others had answered the question, you might have been impressed by some of this 'received opinion'. Nevertheless, in your counter-argument you presented evidence that you believed gave stronger support to your position.

All the same, you might have come to believe that your original intuition was less safe than you'd thought, and perhaps that your argument is less persuasive than you'd hoped. It's no sin to have modified your position, and to come to a less firm conclusion than you'd thought you would. The partial or complete falsification of a hypothesis is often as useful as when it's verified.

In a humanities, even in a social science essay, you won't prove anything; and there is always room for an **alternative conclusion**. Consider this extract from a paper by Polish academic Ewa Rusek, for instance:

English as a Global Language

Nowadays a global language appears to be more necessary than ever. Since World War II, English has been spreading relentlessly, and it is now an international medium of communication. In globalized trade, multinational companies, international travel, and such collective organizations as the World Bank, it simplifies proceedings and cuts the enormous costs of translation.

Unlike Latin and other former common languages, English seems to be too widespread and too deeply rooted to die out in the foreseeable future. English is characterized not only by the matchless number of its native speakers and those who use it as a second language, but also by the number of people willing to master it, its geographical distribution, and its use in international contacts.

The statement attributed to George Bernard Shaw, 'English is the easiest language to speak badly', aptly encapsulates the relative ease with which people beginning to learn English can understand what others say and also make themselves understood. English is a reasonably concise language, not very prone to misunderstandings due to cultural subtleties. In addition, it is democratic in that it has no coding for social differences. It is adaptable and flexible – it has adopted thousands of words from other languages, which gives it a feeling of familiarity.

The conclusion would seem to be that English will maintain its position as *the* global language. But it would not be unreasonable to stake a claim for Mandarin Chinese, the language spoken by the largest number of people in the world, given a boost by the hundreds of new Confucius Institutes; or for Spanish, accounting for the second largest number, and now the second language even of the USA.

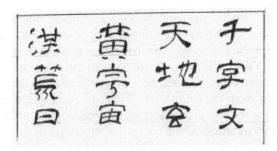

There are always alternative conclusions one might come to, particularly where the future is concerned. It's worth repeating that whatever conclusion you come to, it should be expressed moderately. Understatement is, in general, more persuasive than over-statement.

> I laid emphasis on framing your title as a question. Now that you have 'answered' the question, you might wish to rephrase the title as a statement.

*

You may be required to write an **abstract** of your essay. Though this appears at the beginning, it's best written at the end, when you can be clear about what you've done.

It will consist of just one paragraph. Its object is to give your reader a brief outline of what to expect, covering the following:

- the scope of the work
- the reason for the choice of research question
- how information was collected
- a significant finding
- possible implications of this finding

A few **keywords** are generally listed at the end.

Here's an example, under a by-now familiar title:

Is the rewilding of the countryside more than simple nostalgia?

Abstract: The decision was made to assemble a number of recent cases of rewilding, to determine whether there were good reasons for pursuing the policy. The issue is a pressing one, as climate change raises questions about species diversity, and land use. Cases were collected deemed to have harmful effects, and others deemed to confer benefits. On balance, rewilding is vindicated, as long as plant and animal species are chosen that are appropriate to, and that enhance, the ecosystem. Nostalgia by itself can rarely be a safe or sufficient motive for a rewilding scheme.

Keywords: rewilding, species, ecology, costs and benefits.

> You will note that the pronoun 'I' is not used; and that the passive form of the verb is preferred so as to avoid it.

> There is just one more thing: when you think you've finished, spare time to **read the essay from beginning to end** (and/or get someone else to do it), so that you spot the typos and mis-spellings that you wouldn't want your supervisor to see.
>
> I have re-read the text of this short book several times; but it may yet be that a typo will have slipped through.

Here's a digest of the essay/dissertation/thesis-plan recommended for use:

Let your title be in the form of a **Question** – one that you ask, yourself. This will ensure that your essay is a focused answer, that it is *your* answer, and that whatever material does not answer the question is discarded as irrelevant to your purposes.

Here follows your **Introduction**, or **Statement of Intent**, where (1) you define any ambiguous terms, and (2) delimit the scope of the enquiry. You should (3) state **your own position** in the debate – your hypothesis – and (4) indicate your method of finding information to support your case.

Begin by examining the **Received Opinion (the literature)** on the subject – what has generally been said. By presenting this review first, you acknowledge that there are other points of view than yours. Your thesis will, in effect, be a counter-argument, in which you either dissent from, or add something to, the position that you've reviewed.

→

Your **Counter Argument**: where you lay out your reasons – in a considered order – for disagreeing with the received opinion or finding it inadequate. The strength of your argument will depend upon the *evidence* (the examples, the facts) that you can find to support your position. It needs to be stronger than the evidence for the argument you are rejecting.

You might come to an **Intermediate Conclusion** on the basis of your own evidence, where you consider what possible conclusions might be drawn.

Now for your overall **Conclusion**. It should reflect what you think, having weighed up both sides. It may not be precisely the same as the position you took in your statement of intent, and it may be tentative.

A (short) sample essay

This is not added as an example of a perfect piece of academic writing. It's offered simply as an illustration of how a (probably much longer) argument might be laid out.

Does the fact that we have a concept of evil mean that evil *exists*?

We use the word 'evil' to denote extreme wrong-doing. We say an act is evil when it causes significant harm to, perhaps, large numbers of people, directly or indirectly; and we call the person or persons evil who perform the act. Evil, to this extent, is an idea – a concept – that would appear to be widely shared, because few of us wish to be harmed. For evil to *exist*, though, it has not merely to be an idea: it has to be recognizably 'out there', as it were, as a force of nature.

I shall not, in this essay, consider 'the problem of evil' used as an argument against the existence of a good, all-powerful God. The suffering that there, undoubtedly, is in the world does seem to weaken the argument for a loving and merciful God – but this is a 'problem' for believers only; one that Dawkins (2006: p. 108) claims 'keeps theologians awake at night'. Major causes of the suffering, of course, are natural calamities like earthquakes, floods and the like, and the varieties of disease that humankind is subject to. There are those who might call these events 'evils'; but it is the existence of moral evil that we are concerned with here. The position taken in this essay is that evil does not exist as an identifiable, natural phenomenon. First, though, I shall consider the case for the claim that evil does exist in some palpable form, by examining the word in common usage.

When we think of evil-doers we are likely – at least from a 'western', liberal perspective – to name men (they are all men) like Adolf Hitler, Joseph Stalin, Mao Zedong, Pol Pot, and Osama Bin Laden. Hitler was responsible for the deaths of millions of Jews and uncountable others; Stalin consigned c. 2.7 million Soviet citizens to their deaths in the Gulag (Applebaum, 2003: p. 520); Pol Pot's rule of terror led to the deaths of something like a quarter of Cambodia's population of seven million (Mydans, 1998); and Bin Laden was behind the deaths of almost 3,000 people when the Twin Towers were felled on '9/11'. What entitles us to call these acts evil is that the actors intended all these deaths; they were not an unforeseen accident. The policies of Mao Zedong led to the deaths of many millions of Chinese people in the so-called 'Great Leap Forward' of 1958, and the 'Cultural Revolution' of 1966 (BBC, no date); but these, if we are to be charitable, were unintended consequences of misguided policies. A truly evil act is when one does, or causes others to do, serious harm – and perhaps kill – people with malicious intent. The moral philosopher G. E. Moore (1903: p. 212) wrote: 'The consciousness of intense pain (...) can be maintained to be a great evil'. And a later philosopher, C. E. M. Joad (1937: pp. 92, 93) wrote:

> My reason tells me that calamity and suffering have no purpose whatever – they are, I believe, just part of the evil of the universe, and that the universe does contain real, objective evil (...). I still believe that physical pain is an unmitigated evil, the greatest in the world.

He wrote this when he was in pain, himself. Plainly, in calling pain an 'objective evil', he supposed it to exist. Both men felt that to be in pain was to be subject to evil; and to cause pain was to bring the greatest evil down on someone else.

If to cause pain to – never mind kill – one person is evil, to cause the deaths of many people might be thought a greater evil. It is an evil still greater, surely, when a man is the sole agent of multiple deaths, with an expert knowledge of what he was doing, as the UK physician Dr Harold Shipman was. Shipman was convicted in 2000 of having killed 15 of his elderly patients by administering lethal injections of diamorphine. A public enquiry followed, which published six reports, the last one of which (Hampshire SAB, no date) concluded that he had killed up to 250 patients in a career of killing that might have begun soon after he qualified. A man trained to keep patients alive had, quite systematically, done the opposite. If we cannot call such a man Evil, with a capital E, then perhaps, there is nobody to whom we can attach the word.

When Bishop of Johannesburg Desmond Tutu called *apartheid* 'intrinsically evil', in 1985; when Saddam Hussein of Iraq promised, in 1991, 'the mother of all battles between good and evil', at the approach of the Americans to liberate Kuwait; and when President George W. Bush linked Iraq with Iran and North Korea in an 'axis of evil', in 2002, it seems they all thought of evil as having objective existence. When we use 'evil' as a noun, perhaps we all do. These three men would all have called themselves believers, though, for whom evil might well have evoked images of the devil, of Satan, a being (almost) as 'real' as God, or

Allah. Non-believers are more likely to use the word 'evil' as an adjective to describe something, or someone, as morally abominable.

The problem in the use of the word – especially as a noun – is that it explains nothing. It seems to put an extreme of wrong-doing in an existential category of its own, when right and wrong are matters of degree. Mackie (1990: pp. 15, 38), writes: 'There are no objective values (...) If there were such things as objective values, they'd be queer entities utterly unlike anything else in the universe'. The same can be said of evil.

It seemed to many that the Second World War had unleashed wrong-doing of an altogether unprecedented sort, on an industrial scale. At the Nuremberg Trials of high-ranking Nazis, many of the defendants claimed that they had simply been obeying orders. One such Nazi, Adolf Eichmann, evaded capture until 1960, and was placed on trial in Israel, in 1961. The German philosopher Hannah Arendt was commissioned by *The New Yorker* to report on the trial. Her report of 1963, *Eichmann in Jerusalem: A Report on the Banality of Evil*, judged Eichmann to be a 'terrifyingly normal' bureaucrat. Arendt went on to write, in 1977: 'The sad truth is that most evil is done by people who never make up their minds to be good or evil' (Maden, 2020). In the very same year that Arendt published her report, 1963, Stanley Milgram, a Yale University psychologist, carried out his famous 'obedience experiment' (Encina, 2004). The white-coated experimenter asked members of the public, in turn, to give (bogus) mild-to-severe electric shocks to a 'learner' – in fact, an actor – when he gave the wrong answer to a question whose correct answer he was supposed to have 'learnt'. Most obeyed in spite of evident qualms, as the actor went into pretended spasms, demonstrating that one does not have to be a Nazi to obey the orders of an apparent authority. Together, Arendt and Milgram did much to persuade the world of the 'banality of evil' – of its ordinariness. Perhaps today we rather speak of the banality of mental ill-health. Dylan Klebold, along with Eric Harris, killed 12 students and a teacher and wounded 24 others, at Columbine High School, in Denver, Colorado, in 1999. His mother wrote about the tragedy in a book published 17 years later in which she wrote: 'Dylan was vulnerable in many ways – unquestionably emotionally immature, depressed, possibly suffering from a more serious mood or personality disorder' (Klebold,2016: p. 277).

Human beings are too complex to be written off as evil, as if subject to a force mysteriously 'out there'. Indeed, neuroscience is casting doubt on whether it can be said that we possess free will, suggesting that we are less in control of what we do than our systems of criminal justice have always assumed. Just as we have dispensed with the idea that there is a Devil out there, or that an individual might be possessed of a devil that incantations might exorcise, so it seems we should give up the metaphysical belief in evil as an entity that has an objective existence.

Bibliography

Applebaum, Anne (2003) *Gulag: A History*. London, UK: Penguin Books

BBC (no date) Mao Zedong (1893-1976). Available from: https://www.bbc.co.uk/history/historic_figures/mao_zedong.shtml [Accessed 14 May 2021]

Dawkins, Richard (2006) *The God Delusion*. London, UK: Bantam Books

Encina, Gregorio (2004) Milgram's Experiment on Obedience to Authority. Available from: https://nature.berkeley.edu/ucce50/ag-labor/7article/articla35.htm [Accessed 28 July 2021]

Hampshire Safeguarding Adults Board (no date) Shipman Public Inquiry. Available from: https://www.hampshiresab.org.uk/learning-from-experience-database/serious-case-reviews/shipman... [Accessed 14 May 2021]

Joad, C.E.M Joad (1937) *The Testament of Joad*. London, UK: Faber & Faber Ltd.

Klebold, Sue (2016) *A Mother's Reckoning*. London, UK: W. H. Allen

Mackie, J. L. (1990) *Ethics: Inventing Right and Wrong*. London, UK: Penguin Books

Maden, Jack (2020) Hannah Arendt on Standing up to the Banality of Evil. Available from: https://philosophybreak.com/articles/hannah-arendt-on-standing-up-to-the-banality-of-evil/ [Accessed 14 May 2021]

Moore, G. E. (1903) *Principia Ethica*. Cambridge, UK: Cambridge University Press

Mydans, Seth (1998) Death of Pol Pot. In: *The New York Times*, 17 April 1998

58

Notes

Note 1

English doesn't like long **sentences**. It used to: this sentence in Hilaire Belloc's *Crooked Streets*, on page 14, is quite long, for instance:

> One street marks a boundary, another the channel of an ancient stream, a third the track some animal took to cross a field, hundreds upon hundreds of years ago; another shows where a rich man's garden stopped long before the first ancestor his family can trace was born – the garden is now all houses, and its owner who took delight in it is just a name.

It reads a bit like a list, though, so it hangs together. A modern writer might want a full-stop after 'years ago'. Another rather long sentence is Samuel Johnson's definition of Thunder, on page 19.

The English sentence generally favours the Subject > Verb > Object (SVO) structure – and the sooner this structure comes in the sentence the better. The English reader doesn't want to wait too long for the verb; a sentence isn't a sentence without it.

On the other hand, a text that's *all* short sentences would soon irritate:

> Short sentences. Popular newspapers use them. They make their point quickly. They force themselves on the reader's attention. They have an urgency about them. They shoot from the hip. Today's readers don't have time for long sentences. They want breaking news. They want it fast.

It's relentless. It might work well for a time, but it's too assertive, too bullying. The ideal is a mixture of short and longer sentences – and the short ones might be best at the beginning and at the end of a paragraph. (See also **Note 6**, about starting a sentence with a present participle, *-ing* form, of the verb).

Note 2

One reason for avoiding the first-person singular ('*I* did this, and then *I* did that') is that it quickly looks self-centred. A more important reason, though, is that an academic essay should be *objective*: a considered, dispassionate examination of the evidence for a claim or claims – an argument. Use of the **'I' pronoun** gives the impression of a subjective, rather personal, and almost certainly biased approach.

We all have our biases. We all see the world from our own point of view, and so have a certain angle on it; we have no choice. Alan Isaacs uses the pronoun seven times in three sentences, at the beginning of *The Survival of God in the Scientific Age* (page 20):

> I have attempted to bring together some of the most interesting ideas from a variety of disciplines – physics, biology, psychology, philosophy, and theology (...). I have necessarily had to avoid trying to be exhaustive, so while I have certainly not told the whole truth, I hope that what I have said is nothing but the truth. Even in this respect, though, I am doubtful – as I was trained in only one of these disciplines, there will surely be lapses in the others.

And Sigmund Freud uses it five times in the extract from *The Interpretation of Dreams*, on the same page. Both men do this to make clear their own bias – or, perhaps, rather to be up-front about the limitations of their study. You might need to be similarly honest as you state your position in the introduction to your essay.

You may also want to draw on your **own experience** as you present your evidence to support the claims in your counter-argument. Here, you have no option but to use the I pronoun. You are in your twenties, your thirties, or perhaps older: you have had experience that nobody else has had. You have chosen the theme of your essay because you are interested in it – and your interest may well stem from an already-established familiarity with it. You need not be shy about recalling relevant experience, as long as you are not its primary focus.

Objectivity is the ideal, and it can best be ensured by withholding judgment ('I, therefore, conclude that...') until the conclusion of your essay.

Note 3

I've said, though, that it might be worth drawing on your own experience: I shall now do precisely that. As an adolescent I was something of a republican: I scorned talk of 'Your Majesty', and 'Your Royal Highness', and didn't stand up when the National Anthem was played. Then, as a student at university, I was asked to take part in a

debate about whether the Royal Family should be sent back to Hanover, in Germany, where they'd come from. I was to be the second speaker for the opposition, so I had to argue (against myself) that the monarchy was a 'good thing'.

In the event, as I prepared my speech, I did find reasons for thinking that monarchy might not be such a bad idea. Though, on the one hand:

- the monarchy is expensive to maintain
- the Royal Family sets an unfortunate example of extravagant living
- the hereditary principle does not sit well with democracy
- competence can't be guaranteed across the generations

on the other hand:

- a hereditary monarchy ensures political stability and continuity
- (head-of-state) pomp is separated from (government) power
- the monarchy is a focus of patriotic loyalty
- it commands international respect and tourist income.

It is not easy, though, to argue *for* the received opinion if you find yourself in profound disagreement with it. Over a period of years, I asked Central European students to write an essay in answer to one of a selection of questions. I had talked them through how to write an argumentative essay; and they all had a copy of the chart on page 35 of this book. Nevertheless, having written a satisfactory introduction, most launched into a defence of their own position; if they acknowledged the possibility of an alternative point of view, it featured only as an afterthought.

Objectivity requires you to stand back and take seriously the position that you will argue against, or dissent from in some way. It's worth repeating: an essay/thesis/dissertation is a debate, not a manifesto.

Note 4

Just as sentences were longer in prose written in the past, so too were **paragraphs**. The paragraphs in this book are quite short because I wanted to make points economically. A paragraph is the framework for the making of one point. This point might be framed in one sentence only. Several of the points that I make in this book are made in one sentence.

Online newspaper articles are often presented in one-sentence 'paragraphs', all the way through:

> We tend to hear stories about the worst sort of landlords.

> You know the sort: the ones who refuse to mend a broken window, or raise the rent at the slightest excuse.

> We don't often read about landlords (and ladies) who concern themselves with the welfare of their tenants.

> They do exist, though, and Stella Crowhurst, 48, is one of them.

> She treats her tenants as if they were her friends.

A succession of short paragraphs like this can be just as tedious as a succession of short sentences. The above paragraphs, indeed, aren't paragraphs at all: they're one paragraph consisting of five sentences, separated for easy reading.

A paragraph is a step in an argument, and, ideally, one step – one paragraph – should lead to the next. Edmund Blunden stepped from one paragraph to the next in the extract from *English Villages*, on pages 27, 28:

> (...) It is not for me to praise London or Londoners, or to discuss other of the larger cities in Great Britain, but it must be admitted that in spite of everything, our cities have a way of making friends.

> However this may be, I am persuaded that whoever wishes to find the best in this country, should look in the English village (...)

I have probably broken this 'rule' in many of my own paragraphs in this book.

Note 5

Students for whom English is not their first language often have difficulty with the **definite article**: *the*. I signalled its use on page 19 ('we've used the word "art" to cover so many things...'). I wanted to make the point that 'the' is used before 'word' because it is a particular, or *concrete*, word (specifying 'art'); it wouldn't ordinarily be used before 'art', or 'nature', because these are *abstract* terms. It would only do so if we spoke, for example, of 'the art of flower-arranging', or 'the nature of the beast', where flower-arranging, and the beast, are concrete nouns.

A sound general rule is to use the definite article before a noun that denotes something unique, for example, 'the Scottish Parliament', or 'the paintings of Rembrandt'. (You wouldn't, though, use 'the' directly before a personal, place, or trade name).

Actually, it might be a noun, or an adjective, that *implies* something unique:

- o 'The last novel that she wrote'
- o 'The right thing to do'
- o 'The only solution to the problem'
- o 'The same dress that I was wearing'
- o 'The following few days'

Any comparison between two things or people, and any superlative adjective would normally be preceded by the definite article:

- o 'He's the taller of the twins'; 'this is the more mature of the two trees'
- o 'This is the oldest book in my collection'; 'She's the most intelligent by far'

One reads, in a book review, for instance: 'The poet Isaac Bryson has just written his first novel'. The implication of the definite article is that we know the poet, or that we *should* do – as the reviewer does, or pretends to do. It might have made less of an assumption to write: 'Poet Isaac Bryson...', or 'Isaac Bryson, a poet, has just written...'.

Note 6

I mentioned in **Note 1** that an English sentence generally starts with the subject and is then followed by the verb. On page 20, I wrote:

> Having refined your title and explained what you mean by it, you may still want to limit the scope of the essay.

Here the sentence begins with a verb. I might have written: 'You have refined your essay, and explained...'. This would have made it clear that 'you' were the subject of both parts of the sentence. The subject does need to be the same, before and after the comma.

It can be a tricky structure to get right. Here, a student gets it wrong. (She starts with a subject, a playwright, who is then not the subject of the sentence that follows after the comma):

McGuinness, having been hailed as one of the greatest contemporary playwrights in Ireland, Michael Caven, an acclaimed stage director, comments on McGuinness's success...'

McGuinness is the subject of the first part of the sentence, then the subject switches to Michael Caven after the comma. It would have been better to write: 'McGuinness was hailed as one of the greatest contemporary playwrights in Ireland. Michael Caven, an acclaimed stage director...'. If in doubt, break the one sentence into two, avoiding use of the participle altogether.

Note 7

The verb is what makes a sentence, and it generally comes early on in an English sentence; and an *active* verb is most often preferred to a *passive* one. I wrote 'Let's imagine that you've been assigned this title', on page 22. I could have written, 'Let's imagine that this title has been assigned'. This would switch the subject of the verb, still in the **passive voice**, from 'you' to the 'title', from the personal to the impersonal.

On page 23, under the sub-title 'Describing your methodology', I wrote: 'A random sample of 25 students was asked...'. Here, I switched the subject from 'I' to 'a random sample'. Using the passive voice avoids over-use of the 'I' pronoun. When you state your position in the Introduction, for example, instead of writing: 'I take the view/think/believe that we should keep the monarchy', you might say: 'On balance, there is a lot to be said for keeping the monarchy'. And in describing your methodology, you might write something like this:

An opportunistic sample of 105 people was interviewed in the weeks following the king's death. They were asked to state their age, their gender, and their voting history. Then they were questioned as to what they thought the change to a younger generation of royals might mean. Their responses were recorded in such a way as to assess what correlation, if any, there might be between their opinions and their personal data.

On the whole, though, the active voice is easier to handle. Mishandling the passive voice can lead to a sentence like this: 'The new compensation scheme is hoped to be successful'. Still in the passive voice, the sentence should have been: 'It is hoped that the new compensation scheme will be successful'.

Another mishandled passive sentence recently seen was this one: 'The cottage is comprised of six rooms altogether'. 'Comprise' is a *transitive* verb: this means that it takes a direct object. There was no need for the passive voice. The sentence should have read: 'The cottage comprises six rooms altogether'.

Stick to the active form of the verb where you can.

Note 8

Though the poet Edmund Blunden wrote *English Villages* in 1942 (page 27), I introduced him in the **present tense** ('Edmund Blunden begins an essay on villages...'). In the same way, though Barbara Ward wrote *The Home of Man* in 1976 (page 28), I used the present tense again ('Barbara Ward does something similar when she writes...'). It's fair to say that she probably would have written under a title today that was more gender-inclusive.

In describing your methodology, you will use the past tense; in recording the received opinions of this and that previous writer who has written on your chosen topic, the convention is to use the present tense.

A typical paragraph might look like this:

> Scott (1996) writes approvingly of placing wind turbines inland. Porter (2012), on the other hand writes from experience of turbines in his own backyard: 'They are noisy and intrusive in other ways. What is more, they are a hazard to migrating birds.' He is perfectly at ease with their being placed offshore, though Scott acknowledges the problem that this may pose to fishermen.

You won't want to use 'writes' too much, though; English doesn't like too much verbal repetition. It's best to vary the words you use. Here are a few suggestions for alternative ways of saying much the same thing:

- o   As X explains, ...
- o   As Y makes clear: ...
- o   She puts this as follows: ...
- o   He takes the view that...
- o   On the other hand, X argues that...
- o   X disagrees: she claims that...
- o   It is Y's judgment that...

- o He states boldly that…
- o X agrees with Y that…
- o They put forward the idea that…
- o In response, X maintains that…
- o Whilst Y contends that…
- o He even insists, against this view, that…
- o Y points out that…
- o X acknowledges that Y has a point.

'X writes that' is perfectly fine, though, as long as this formula isn't used too often in the same paragraph.

Note 9

While we're still talking about verbs, it is worth considering the **infinitive** part of the verb and its place in a sentence. The infinitive ('to change', 'to love', 'to prefer') is that part of the verb that remains the same no matter who the subject is ('who changes', 'who loves', 'who prefers') no matter the tense, and no matter whether the verb is negative or positive.

It's the part of the verb that can stand alone, as in: 'To protest was to put oneself in danger; not to do so was, in effect, to support the regime'.

The infinitive in English consists of two words; in other languages it is just one word. 'To go' in Greek is *ienai*; in Latin it is *īre*. Because it was just one word in these classical languages, it was considered by those who laid down the rules of English grammar that the English infinitive should not be split: one should not write (or say) 'to boldly go'; one should say 'to go boldly'. In many other ways, though, English grammar is very different from Greek and Latin grammar, so the split infinitive is nowadays less disapproved of.

Nevertheless, I was surprised to see in a university bulletin that I received recently, the following three instances of the split infinitive:

'It is our aim to quickly create a system to deal with this.'

'We hadn't expected it to spectacularly reveal what had happened'

'Fortunately, we were able to immediately identify the problems'

All three sentences sound awkward. The 'quickly' would have been better placed after 'this'; 'spectacularly' would have been better placed (preceded by 'so') after reveal; and 'immediately', at the end of the sentence.

When one verb follows immediately after another, the second is often infinitive. Thus, we write (and say):

'We tried to change his mind',

'We are trying to change his mind', and

'We tried not to change his mind, but to understand it'

Yet, when the form of the verb is 'try', it's often followed by *and*. We see (and hear): 'We'll try *and* change his mind', It's as if, when we say to a friend: 'Try *and* come if you can', we are asking that friend to do two things: first 'try', and then 'come'. It isn't important – but the 'and' is illogical, and best avoided.

Note 10

There is much about the English language that is illogical – and there is much that seems to be a matter of choice. It isn't always obvious, for example, when one should use a **singular or plural form**. At first, on page 32, I wrote:

'Articles written by even only one named author *is* preferable to one that's anonymous'

Only later did I note that the subject of the sentence is 'articles' – plural – and that the verb should, therefore, be plural also: *are*. Perhaps I was led astray by the repeated use of the word 'one'.

On page 34, I wrote:

'It's vital that you have access to the most recent information coming from a well-established institution (a university, a democratic government, a respected thinktank), or a trustworthy, named individual who *uses* language with care.'

Should that have been 'use'? After all, there is more than one subject of the verb.

The three institutions mentioned in brackets are examples of collective nouns. Others are 'family', 'police', and 'company'. Does one write: 'My family *is* very talented', or 'My family *are* very talented'? It would seem to be a matter of choice. Is it a matter of choice in this example (one frequently seen)?

'These kind of things always irritate'

Shouldn't it be 'this kind of thing always irritates', or 'these kinds of things always irritate'?

Then I saw this quotation from a UK government minister in a quality newspaper:

"I hope Brussels are listening to this conversation and other conversations."

Would the minister have used the plural of the verb 'to be' if the city had been London (or another capital that doesn't end with an 's')?

Finally, while we're talking about plurals, it is worth pointing out that certain abstract, (or uncountable), nouns generally don't take a plural form. 'Damage', for example, as in 'Ukraine suffered widespread damage' – 'damages' are redress for reputational damage in a libel case. 'Training', and 'research' are other examples. It is usual to refer to training courses, and research studies.

Note 11

It's often the short words that confuse students and that, therefore, students confuse. I refer to **prepositions**. These are linking words giving us the where, when, and how of things. There are those about which there is little doubt: *behind, under, above, towards, before, after*. They describe a definite relation in time or place.

The monosyllabic prepositions are more of a problem. Here are some examples:

- o 'I'll come *at* 4.00 o'clock'; 'meet me *at* the station'
- o 'I saw him *in* the lift'; 'it was *in* the morning'
- o 'He'd come *by* bus'; 'he left a note *by* the gate'
- o 'It was *on* Channel 4; 'I watch it *on* Wednesdays'
- o 'You're safe *with* me'; 'do handle it *with* care'
- o 'The aim *of* the research'; 'it was in the year *of* his death'

○ 'It's a short walk *from* here'; 'tell one *from* another'

There are few rules that one can learn; but there are meanings in the madness. An American might say: 'I saw a different film than that one', whereas a native English speaker might well say: 'I saw a different film to that one'. Logically, it should be: 'I saw a different film *from* that one'. After all, we would probably say: 'This one differs *from* that one', just as we'd say: 'this is separate *from* that'.

The prepositions 'to' and 'for' are often confused. The difference between 'doing something *for* someone', and 'doing something *to* someone' is generally clear; but you might have doubts about where to use 'to' and 'for' in the following:

> She gave me the medicine, saying it would be good ...(1)...me. She was here ...(2)... three weeks, and throughout was very good ...(3)... me; I am most grateful ...(4)... her ...(5)... all that she did.

Numbers 1, 2, and 5 are 'for'; and numbers 3 and 4 are 'to'. If in doubt, you will find numerous examples scattered through the text of this book. On page 38, for instance, under the sub-title, you'll find: '*in* the section *on* Sources'; 'read free *of* charge'; 'words *from* a source'; and 'Sumner, *for* one, doubts it'.

Prepositions are often part of a verb (where they're, technically, postpositions): in the same part of page 38, for instance, you will find 'refer to', 'look for', 'pin on', and 'seek after'. Such combinations have to be learnt by rote – you very likely had to learn them like this, cursing as you did so.

Note 12

I have said that English is an illogical language: it is certainly inconsistent in respect of its **spelling**, and how words should be pronounced. The word 'alphabet', for instance, comes to us from Greek (the first two letters of whose alphabet, are *alpha* and *beta*), along with the words 'bibliography', and 'philosophy', on the same page (39). Many of our academic terms (all those *-ologies*, for example) come from Greek. The word 'plagiarism' comes from Greek, too: its original meaning was 'kidnapping'.

English has always been a kidnapping language. It has kidnapped words from a number of other languages, as well as evolving from its own roots in Anglo-Saxon. Anglo-Saxon, or Old English, words tended to be monosyllabic. Those from Latin, coming to us through French, were more often polysyllabic. Here are some examples:

- o Anglo-Saxon (king, pig, lord)
- o Latin (atrocity, futile, obvious – and many, many more)
- o Norman French (homage, cavalry, abbey – and, again, many more)
- o Arabic (turban, zero, tulip)
- o Dutch (harpoon, buoy, yacht)
- o German (zeitgeist, plunder, kindergarten)
- o Spanish (canyon, stampede, mosquito)
- o Hindi (bungalow, pyjamas, chutney)
- o Later French (chandelier, bourgeois, entrepreneur)

It's hardly surprising, therefore, that English spelling and pronunciation are so unpredictable. It's wise never to be too far from a dictionary – or, come to that, a thesaurus.

Note 13

The language is still evolving, of course. I flagged the word 'rewilding' on page 25ff (or should it still be hyphenated: 're-wilding'?) because it is a relatively new word. It appears to have been used first in the early 1990s. Not only do speakers and writers (perhaps most often writers) introduce new words, or new word combinations, they make 'mistakes' that stick.

We used to say of someone that he was 'over-confident', or that a dish was 'over-cooked', where 'over' was an adverb tacked on to an adjective (with or without a hyphen). Who was it who first added an 'ly' to the word, and wrote that that someone was 'overly confident', and the dish 'overly cooked'? (I have also seen 'oftenly', and 'fastly'. Often and fast are, of course, adverbs already).

Things are happening to the past tense of certain verbs:

- o 'To sink' is an irregular verb, whose simple past is 'sank', and whose past participle is 'sunk' ('the ship has sunk').

Increasingly, one is seeing: 'the boat sunk'[19]. The same thing is happening to the verb 'to sing';

- If 'to learn' was treated regularly, we would write: 'I learn*ed* German while I lived in Dresden', and 'I have lear*nt* French already'; but we read and hear: 'I learnt', and 'I have learned'. The same goes for the verb 'to dream'.

- The verb 'to wreak' is an unusual one, but it features in the phrase 'to wreak havoc'. The simple past and the participle of the verb is, or was, 'wrought', (as in 'he wrought wonders', and 'wrought iron'). Now it is being regularized, as in: 'It was damage wreaked by the storm'.

You might think it wise to stick to the original forms in these cases. You might also prefer: "You'd come more quickly if you came by plane", to "You'd come quicker…"; and "I breathe a little more easily now", to "I breathe a little easier now". Am I being pedantic? Possibly. I am unsure how many of these sorts of changes are acceptable – but your supervisor may have a definite preference for qualifying a verb with an adverb, rather than a comparative adjective.

Note 14

'Schalskopf'? It appears to mean either 'bowl-head', or 'empty-head', or, perhaps 'empty-bowl head'. It might be best translated as blockhead, or airhead. Mencken's family was German, and he spoke the language when he was a child. As well as being a journalist, he was a scholar of American English.

You may be studying, yourself, in an institution that favours the use either of British English or American English. You'll be expected, therefore, to be consistent in the use of either one or the other: to spell the word 'defence', or 'defense' (as Mencken does). Interestingly, the final word of the extract is spelt in the British fashion, with the '-our', as opposed to the '-or' ending.

It doesn't much matter whether you use:

- 'colour' or 'color'
- 'organise', or 'organize'
- 'centre' or 'center'

---

[19] Having said this, I have just seen 'sunk' used as the simple past in *The Pickwick Papers*, by Charles Dickens, published in 1836.

- o 'to practise' or 'to practice'
- o 'rumpus' or 'ruckus'
- o 'peep' or 'peek'

What matters is that you are consistent (and attentive to the usual practice in your institution).

It might matter, though, when, in American English one word is used where British English has two. On page 50, I wrote: 'There is always room for an *alternative* conclusion', meaning that there are other conclusions that one might come to on the basis of the same information. In American English, the word used would very likely be *alternate* – but in British English, 'alternate' has a different use altogether, as in: 'Cars may only enter the inner-city zone on *alternate* days, depending on whether their registration plates end with an even or an odd number'.

'Pry' is another word in American English that means both what it means in British English (to inquire rather nosily), and 'prise' (to open forcibly, as in: 'He prised open the oyster to see whether or not there was a pearl inside'). But, perhaps, you are unlikely to need to use either word in your long essay.

Note 15

It is worth saying something, briefly, about **punctuation**. I wrote this on page 46: 'Mary Coleridge was writing in the late 1800s. Here, she writes about explorers in general; but she praises one in particular – a woman like herself – Isabella Lucy Bird, the first woman to join the Royal Geographical Society, in 1892:' In this short paragraph, I used a full-stop; a semi-colon, three commas, two dashes, and a colon. Each has its uses, but the full-stop and comma are more important than the others.

- o The *full-stop* (or 'period' if you're using American English) is what completes the sentence. I made the point, under **Note 1**, that there are writers who use too few full-stops, and there are others who use too many – a balance is best;
- o the *comma* marks a pause between one word, or phrase, or clause, and another. I am inclined to be quite generous with commas in the hope that they add to the readability of a text;
- o the *semi-colon* is a little stronger than a comma, but less strong than a full-stop. It separates two ideas, but combines them in the same sentence if they're closely related: for example, if

they suggest a comparison or contrast ('She was a great writer; it was in her private life that she fell short');

o a *colon* introduces an idea, a quotation, or list, for example: 'There are two ways of looking at this problem: one is to delegate it; the other is to ignore it'. A full-stop would be too much of an intrusion, whilst a comma would not mark a sufficient break;

o some writers don't use the *dash* at all. Dashes do have two functions, though: they can be used instead of brackets, in which case they come in pairs (as in the sentence about Mary Coleridge); or a single dash can attach, as it were, an after-thought to a sentence, as in this example: 'Churchill thought through the consequences of each of his decisions – except, that is, when he failed to do so.'

The above are not rules. They are guidance, only.

Note 16

I said of Mencken's claim concerning a desirable mixture of masculine and feminine characteristics (on page 46) that: 'It's a **generalization**, and there may be some truth in it.' We have to generalize some of the time: we wouldn't say anything very worthwhile if we didn't. If we only spoke in terms of particular instances, we wouldn't learn anything from them. You will generalize when you sum up the 'received opinion'; and you will generalize in your conclusion, having weighed up the evidence for both sides in the debate.

To be avoided are *unsupported* generalization, and *over*-generalization. You would over-generalize, for instance, if you were to write:

o 'All high-achievers have suffered some misfortune in their lives',
o 'Nobody who has achieved anything in life has escaped some misfortune', or
o 'Achievement is never possible unless there has been some misfortune'

Just one individual who has enjoyed uninterrupted good fortune, yet has achieved something, gives the lie to the over-confident 'all', or 'nobody'. If you can't think of an exception to your over-generalization, your supervisor will.

It's generally wise to be tentative, and to use words like: 'some', 'many', even 'most people', in preference to 'all', or 'everyone'; and 'rarely', 'hardly ever', or 'infrequently', in preference to 'never'.

Index

ibidem.eu